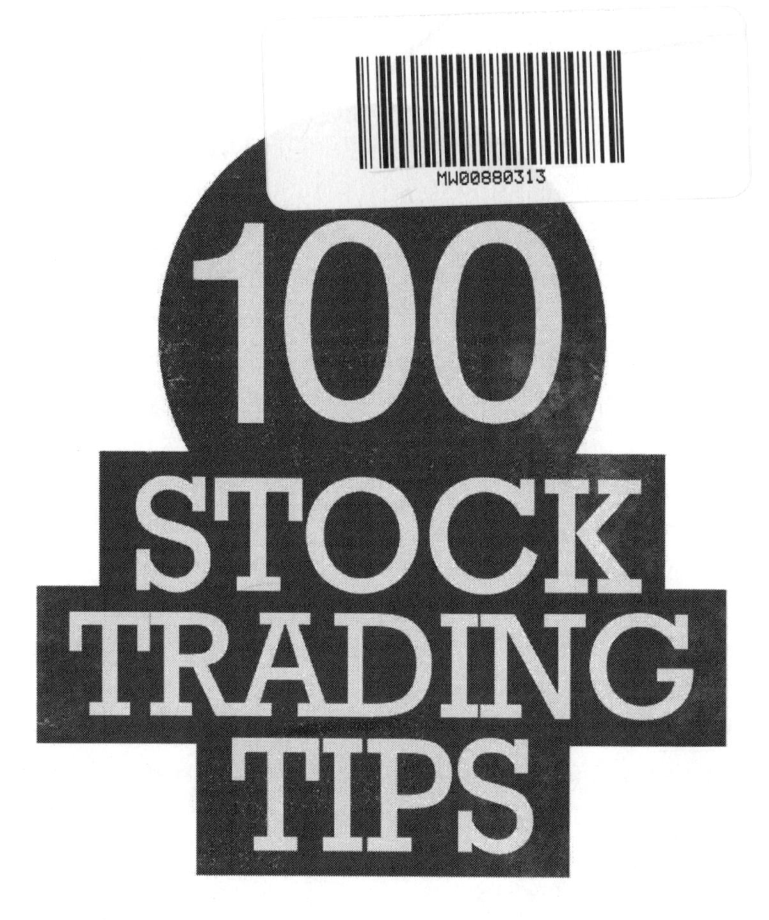

THE MINDSETS YOU MUST KNOW TO BE A PROFITABLE TRADER!

SASHA EVDAKOV

INTRODUCTION

"Trade stocks: make fast money and make a fortune." This is what most people think when it comes to trading stocks in the stock market. Over the years I have seen more traders become broke than a swarm of wasps dropping dead after being sprayed with pesticide.

Many people want quick riches and that's what they hope to find in the stock market. This is not how things work in the markets and you need to understand that the odds are stacked against you due to high frequency traders and market professionals. Although you can make a great fortune in the stock market you must be determined, patient, persistent, and you have to be willing to do some difficult things internally. However most cannot stick with it long enough to see their results come to fruition or aren't willing to do the necessary things to achieve their dreams.

Before you get into the markets you have an enormous amount of study and work. Almost as much as a doctor. Your study may consist of eight years of gruesome nights until you become a professional. It's not going to happen overnight.

Consider that a tennis player isn't created overnight. It takes years for them to become great. After practicing ten plus years on the tennis court then they may become a professional and win their million dollar tournaments. This is similar to the stock market.

Little victories and tournaments do come. If you are looking for the big wins right from the beginning your thinking process is incorrect and you should adjust it quickly or else you will be disappointed.

As for my early years in trading I first got into the stock market when I was about 14 years old. My mom was the one who introduced me to the markets. Although I had heard about them before it was because of her that I became interested in stocks.

At the time she worked as a private health care nurse to older patients in Florida and they were always watching their stocks and checking their investments. Slowly after about five years of watching the markets with her patients my mom decided to try trading some stocks.

I helped her open the account and then I did the trading, but she would tell me the picks of what and when to buy or sell.

The first year was great! We traded one stock in particular – where we made a few hundred dollars profit weekly. It was a good feeling making an extra $1000 a month!

After some time I took the reins into my own hands. I got the investment capital to trade from working on my digital design business. After about six months of isolated gains I hit a critical part in my trading. I lost over $16,000 in about 16 minutes!!! It was a biotech company and really proved to me that I had no clue what I was doing.

I decided to take a moment to step back and try to figure out what had happened. From then on I took the next 7+ years to just study everything I could get my hands on and slowly made my way back to the market. It took a major experience to realize how fast I could lose money in the markets.

Since that time I put many disciplines in place and created my own trading system. I decided to help other people out with the knowledge that I had learned when I started my educational business. Stock market education was expensive and I wanted to give everyone the opportunity to learn what I learned over the last 10+ years.

That's my goal for you. Learn what you can and then make it your own. Make your money work for you! Think of each dollar as a little worker that is out there working for you.

In this book I want to share with you the quick tips and mindsets that you can use to transform your trading style, get insight, learn more, or get a different perspective so you can stay profitable.

This book is not about giving you the Bible to stock trading. It's about giving you tidbits to think about during the day while you are trading. You can use this book and read one new page each trading day or you can read through it, digest it, and create or revise your own trading system.

TRADING DISCLAIMER

Sasha Evdakov or Rise2Learn, LLC are NOT licensed financial advisers (here will be referred to as Rise2Learn). Nothing contained in our material (hereinafter referred to as media) is intended to be or construed to be as financial advice. All information on any media is not intended as investment, tax, accounting, or legal advice. Nor is it an offer or endorsement or recommendation of any company, security, or fund.

TRADING INVOLVES RISK AND IS NOT SUITABLE FOR ALL INVESTORS

Online trading has inherent risk due to system response and access times that may vary due to market conditions, system performance, and other factors. An investor should understand these and additional risks before trading. While implied volatility represents the consensus of the marketplace as to the future level of stock price volatility or probability of researching a specific price point there is no guarantee that this forecast will be correct.

Content, research, tools, and stock or option symbols are for entertainment, educational, and illustrative purposes only and do not imply a recommendation or solicitation to buy or sell a particular security or to engage in any particular investment strategy. The projections or other information regarding the likelihood of various investment outcomes are hypothetical in nature, and are not guarantees of future results.

You agree that all content including all media under Rise2Learn, LLC along with its materials are proprietary rights and that their use is restricted by the terms of this agreement. Use of the content, media, or material, for any purpose without written permission from Rise2Learn, LLC is strictly prohibited. You further agree that you will not create derivate works of this media, material or products offered by Rise2Learn, LLC.

Rise2Learn does not guarantee or promise any income or particular result from your use of the information contained herein. Rise2Learn, LLC assumes no responsibility or liability for issues, errors, or omissions in the information in our media.

DAMAGES AND LIABILITIES

Rise2Learn will not be liable for any incidental, indirect, direct, punitive, consequential, special, exemplary, or other damages including, but not limited to, loss of revenue or income, pain and suffering, emotional distress, or similar damages even if Rise2Learn has been advised of the possibility of such damages.

In no event will the collective liability to any party (regardless of the form of action, whether in contract, tort, or otherwise) exceed the greater of $100 or the amount you have paid to Rise2Learn for the information product, service, seminar, or media out of which liability arose. Under no circumstances will Rise2Learn be liable for any loss or damage caused by your reliance on the information contained herein.

It is your responsibility to evaluate the accuracy, completeness, or usefulness of any information, advice, opinion, or other content contained in any media presented by Rise2Learn. Please seek the advice of professionals, as appropriate, regarding the evaluation of any specific information, advice, opinion, or content, or media.

COPYRIGHT NOTICE

This book is copyright. I love spreading knowledge in the world, educating other people, and helping others achieve their potential. You are welcome to cite things from this book however please give credit back to me or my website http://tradersfly.com or http://sashaevdakov.com.

If you have any questions regarding the copyright or would like to use parts of it on your website, presentation, just contact me from my stock trading website http://tradersfly.com or my personal website http://sashaevdakov.com

COPYRIGHT FROM THE LAWYERS

Please do **not** distribute, copy, or create derivate works of this book as this book as it contains material protected under International and Federal Copyright Laws and Treaties. Any unauthorized reprint or use of this material is prohibited. No part of this book may be reproduced or transmitted in any form or by any means, electronic or mechanical, including photocopying, recording, or by any information storage and retrieval system without express written permission from the author / publisher.

Okay, enough with that. Let's get into some stock market tips!

RESOURCES

Before you get too far I just want to give you a few handful resources that I use. All of these resources can be easily found on my website at:

http://tradersfly.com : Free Stock Trading Lessons
http://sashaevdakov.com : My personal / business website

If you visit www.tradersfly.com there are a plethora of articles, videos, and resources to learn from. Most of them are free! If you decide to take your trading to the next level and want to accelerate your education I have created in depth video training material that are unlike any others on the market.

With that being said... let's get rolling!

You can spend your day trading the markets or spend it with your family. Remember that every day is expensive and there is more to life than the market.

Every day is expensive as heck when you think of it from the world's perspective. You are giving your life to each and every single day! You can choose to spend the day on learning the markets, trading, or you can spend the time with your family. Bad days will come in the markets. You can't avoid them. However, if you know your purpose in life then you know what to do when the markets are idle.

Ask yourself what would you do if you had an extra $5,000,000 in your bank account right now? Would you choose to spend it with your family? Or would you choose to play with your toys like a motorcycle?

If your answer doesn't involve spending it in front of the computer screen then go out and do what makes you happy. When the markets aren't acting right for your trading style then go out and enjoy those things that you love to do. Take some time to go to the beach, spend time with your family, or read a great book. The markets will be there long after we are all gone.

You can control the day or the day will control you. You get to choose.

Sometimes emotions can run wild when you trade stocks. When the market is not acting in your favor and you get emotional then the market is controlling you.

If you are not in control of your decisions, your choices will be irrational. It's at this point where you will lose large amounts of your capital.

Learn to control your emotions, think clearer, and be more level-headed because your outcome in the markets will be reflected based on you.

The inner-battle you are facing is only with yourself.

If you always continue to do the same thing you will always get the same results.

If you constantly go to bed late, but have to wake up early you will always be tired. It's a loop cycle that we get wrapped up in. Similar to how people typically date the same people, eat the same foods, dress the same way. We like repetition and we like our comfort zone.

If you are repeatedly taking losses and a few wins during certain times you will justify that it's okay because you do get some wins. However you are in this loop cycle of constantly taking losses – so the results you get will always be the same until you make changes.

If you want to change your results you need to change your actions and that is one of the hardest things for people to do. Try changing your daily routine for one day or what you wear such as from non-dressy to dressy. Get a new friend to hang out with for the day.

It is difficult to change quickly, but the better you get at it the more versatile and flexible you will be in your trading.

Success is nothing more than doing a few simple things every single day.

If you want to be successful in anything you need to continue doing the right things to get to your desired outcome. If you want to become a professional tennis player you need to practice daily for a few hours. After 10 years go out and win your monster tournament and collect your sponsorship earnings.

If you want to be a professional stock trader, you need to focus on stock trading for multiple days out of the week for years and continue to improve your game. It isn't something that you can do as a weekend activity. It takes years of practice to become successful. However, if you do the right things over the years you will eventually get to your desired outcome.

Remember the top sports players make millions of dollars. The top hedge fund managers make billions of dollars. There is money in this industry.

Usually summer time is slow for the markets. All the rich folks are at their summer homes in the Hamptons. Learn to read the summer tape.

Trading during the summer months can be different than what people normally expect. Volume during the summer is weaker because all the rich folks go to the Hamptons to their summer home and relax.

They are less active in the markets and when they are less active then the market slows down since they are the ones running the show.

If you are still planning to trade during the summer months understand that volume may appear lower than the average during the summer, but this movement may still be healthy. It may take a few summer seasons of trading for you to understand the behavior during the summer months, but you'll get it.

You will suffer the pain of discipline or the pain of regret. Which do you choose?

You can choose one of two pains when it comes to trading stocks: the pain of discipline or the pain of regret. If you are one who wants to trade every stock and jump on every trade possible you will suffer from the pain of regret. Your failures and extreme losses will put you in a state of regret and you will wonder at times "what happened?"

On the flip side if you are someone who is patient and allows a stock chart to set up then you will suffer from the pain of discipline because it will be difficult to sit and wait for the right setups - especially at the beginning. We humans always want that instant gratification so it is quite unnatural to be patient.

The important point is that you get to choose whether you want to learn from the pain of discipline or the pain of regret. So which do you choose?

No one has a crystal ball for the markets. The only thing you can rely on is your cash and your stops.

The markets are very unpredictable. No one has a crystal ball out there to tell them what will happen in the future. If they did, they wouldn't tell you anyways because they would be busy placing trades based on what the crystal ball told them.

You can't rely on other people's predictions and what they say because their chances of being right are the same as yours. The only difference is that you might *feel* they have more credibility because they are on TV, but it doesn't make a difference.

The only thing you can count on is your cash and your stops so always listen to your game plan. Your cash are your players and your stops are your blockers to protect your players from getting hurt.

If you want to do something you will figure it out. If you don't - then you will find an excuse.

When you are serious about learning to trading stocks or transforming yourself into a better trader then you will continue to push yourself to be better.

People who are successful do not always know the exact steps it takes to reach their success, but in their minds they know that if they do not understand something, they will figure it out.

People who are not serious about their future will typically create an excuse on why something did not work in their favor. They will have an excuse on why they are overweight, why they are broke, or why their trading profits are horrible.

Don't make up excuses. Be the one that figures things out!

Learn to sit and wait for the right setups. Don't be like a druggie looking for your next fix.

You know how drug addicts are constantly looking for their next fix because they can't get enough of the rush? They are always in search for where they can get their next high because they can't live without it. This is how some people act when they are trading stocks.

They want to constantly trade even if they just had a huge win or a huge loss. Typically there is a rush mentality that sets in after a win where people want another one because they feel lucky or powerful. On the flip side, if you take a loss you want to jump back in to make up for that loss and you get the "I can get it back mentality."

In stocks you need sit and wait for the right setup. It isn't about jumping into every trade you can when you want to. It's about letting the market take the appropriate action and come to you so you can step in the bus and enjoy the ride when the bus stops in front of you.

Don't be a stock market druggie because you will always be in search of your next stock trading high.

Technicals will always trump fundamentals because fundamentals will not hold up a stock if everyone wants to get out.

Stocks may have great fundamentals, but charts and technicals will always trump a stock's fundamentals.

When panic sets in and the big institutions want to get out of the stock - the fundamentals do not apply. At this point people are trading on fear and not on company data. They are looking to protect their profits.

This can be a great time to make an obscene amount of money if you are calm and wait for the opportunity. However remember that you can't trade on fundamentals if things are in a panic. You need to just step aside and let the market take its course until things setup in your favor.

If you don't design your life plan you will fall into someone else's life plan.

The person who will care the most about your money is YOU!

If you don't create a plan that fits with your vision then you will fall into someone else's plan. How much will they care about you? Not much.

Design a plan that fits your lifestyle and your goals so that you can achieve greatness. This can be something as simple as raising your capital amount invested after each profitable month.

For example, the first month you may have $10,000 in your portfolio. The second month you may add $3,000 if you were profitable. This could continue until trading becomes a full-time activity for you.

Design a plan for yourself. Go after what you want!

Don't over analyze things in the stock market. It will only cloud your judgment.

Analysis paralysis happens to all of us - even the greatest traders. If you start to overanalyze a stock then skip the trade. Overanalyzing will only cloud your judgment when it comes to a stock. Your brain will start to play tricks on you about when to enter, how much to trade, and if the stock is acting right. You don't need mind games when it comes to your trades.

Keep things as simple as possible and don't overanalyze your stock trades. It is for this reason I don't like to trade with 50 indicators on my screen like some people. Watch one or two indicators at most and learn to trade off of them exceptionally well. You don't want to confuse yourself. There are too many other things in the world that will confuse you.

Sometimes the best position to play is all in cash.

The stock market will not always have great days, weeks, months, or years. Certain times you will be able to spot great opportunities and other times you will not.

Your trading opportunities will be determined based on your experience as well as the type of trader you are. For example if you only trade long in the markets and we have a 9 month bear market then during those months you should trade minimally or not at all.

The more experience you have in the markets the better you will be able to spot opportunities and take advantage of them when they arrive. If you do not see any great opportunities then the best position to play is in cash.

You make more money when you learn to be patient than when you have an itchy trading finger.

Patience and waiting for the right time to enter a stock pays. Imagine you were cooking and every time a crumb fell on the floor you had to bend over and pick it up. This is not very efficient - it is stressful and mentally draining. For efficiency it is better to clean up your kitchen once you are done cooking rather than to bend over and clean the floor each time.

When it comes to trading stocks, you don't need to trade every single minute with every single slight move in the stock price trying to capture that 50 cent gain. Instead wait for the large setups that are setting up to breakout $20, $50, or $100 move.

This is how you can keep your sanity and stay profitable. An itchy trigger finger does not pay well.

When a stock breaks a trend line you don't have to be the first one to get in.

As you watch support, resistance, and trend lines closely you will be anticipating the breakout. Stocks don't hit these lines perfectly. There is always confluence where the stock bounces around these ranges. In essence this means you don't have to be the first one to get in the stock when it breaks out. Allow it to confirm the move and then get in. Make sure that the odds are in your favor!

Stocks can move up on lighter volume & they are tradable. If a stock moves up on lighter volume then the pull back is usually stronger when it comes.

Volume is the key for indicating that a stocks movement is real however this doesn't mean a stock can't move up on lighter volume. Can a car be moved forward if it has a blown engine? Of course it can! You can tow it or push it. However eventually it will need a working engine to operate properly.

Stocks are very similar. It is better if a stock has heavy volume to the upside and lighter volume on pull backs. That implies a move is healthy. A stock moving up on lighter volume is tradable. Just understand that when the pull-back happens it will be faster than if it was a healthy move.

For this reason, a stock that is testing its highs on light volume is usually not successful to breaking out to a new range. These stocks are typically great short opportunities at their highs.

Think of them like little kids trying to make a slam dunk on a ten foot professional basketball hoop - most of them will never reach it.

The more familiar you are with the stock the more successful you will be at predicting its movement.

If you learn how to drive a Ferrari very well you will get to your destination faster than if you drive a tractor. However a Ferrari cannot pull lumber through the forest. A Ferrari moves differently than a tractor just like Google moves differently than McDonald's stock.

When you learn the behavior of stocks and anticipate their movement you will be far more successful.

Ride the wave that comes your way and stay on as long as you can.

When you are trading stocks to the upside or downside often times people talk about targets. If you have targets, you may limit your profits. Instead, look to ride the stock as long as possible so that you can capture the maximum gain.

Think of riding the stocks like a surfer rides a wave. You get on the wave and stay on as long as possible until the ride is over.

You don't jump off the surf board if you feel comfortable, stable, and everything is going smoothly. Instead you hang on until the end.

Do the same with stocks and ride them for as long as possible.

When the big boys and institutions want to get out the door is never big enough.

It takes the big institutions months to accumulate a position since they have billions of dollars and shares that they need to purchase. They can't do it overnight to acquire all these shares because they would move the stock too much.

After their accumulation period and the stock rises, they slowly start selling part of their position. They do it in small quantities in hopes of not taking the stock down too far too fast.

However, when a huge selloff happens they are forced to dump the shares to the open market in order to avoid holding bad stock.

Since they have to dump and get rid of millions of shares in the open market there are never enough buyers to take their shares.

For this reason the stock goes down hard and fast because there are not enough buyers at the higher prices. It is a small door to push all those shares through.

Always aim to gauge where prices want to go to the upside or the downside. You will get a better idea of what moves are realistic or unrealistic.

You can pray or hope that your stock will go up forever, but from experience stock prices rarely go up for a long time quickly.

As you learn to read chart patterns you will start seeing what moves are realistic in stocks over a few days, a few weeks, or in a month.

As you get better at predicting realistic moves you will be able to spot how far a stock can go. This will give you an insight of when to take your money off the table or reduce your risk.

If you get lucky and the stock continues to run higher you don't have to panic or get ecstatic. Just be cautious because it can reverse at any time especially if it hits its projected move.

Focus on trading stocks that are the leaders – not the penny stocks.

This is what the institutions trade because they move the fastest and have the greatest liquidity. If you want to be good, and I mean really good, you need to learn how to trade the leaders and the high dollar stocks.

Trading penny stocks can still be great, but they move $1 to $3 on a great day. The leaders move $1 to $3 dollars on a bad day. On a great day they move $7 to $15.

Yes it may be more difficult to get a lot of shares when you are first starting out if you trade the leaders, but once you are successful if you put in $300,000 into a penny stock you will be stuck trying to get out. Their volume is limited and you will move the stock too much. When you trade the leaders you have more flexibility and liquidity.

There is a reason why they are called the leaders. Not to mention I've never seen a penny stock move 50+ points in a week whereas Google, Apple, and Priceline have done it multiple times per year!

You don't have to trade every day to make a living. You just have to trade the right stocks at the right time, have a plan, and stick to your plan.

When I first started trading stocks I wanted to trade every single stock I could and I wanted to do it every day! Gosh was that a horrible idea! In order to be successful at this business you need to trade the right stocks at the right time. Trading more often will just bring you stress.

Instead, enjoy your life and what your money can do for you and for the people around you. Wait for the right setups so that you can capture the nice runs in stocks when they are breaking out.

If you wait for the setups you may only have to trade a few weeks or months out of the year. The rest of the time you can just go on vacation and take it easy.

Wouldn't that be nice?

Don't think about your profits.
Money comes when you learn to manage your risk.

I often run into traders that always focus on their potential or possible profits before or after they enter the trade. This can be a huge mistake and a disaster. It's like focusing on your sex life during a math exam. It is a nice thought and daydream, but it won't help you with your math exam.

Your profits will grow as a trader when you focus on managing your risk.

I know that we want to think of the possibilities, the things we can buy, and how many trades it will take us to get there when we first start out – but don't do that! It will steal your focus from what's important. The end result will give you losing trades.

Take profits into strength as the stock moves in your favor. You will be more profitable.

Stocks never go straight up nor do they move the way you want them to move. Since you can't control a stock's movement or direction you need to always take profits as it is moving in your favor.

This doesn't mean you have to sell everything you have in a short gain. It means that you can sell 100 shares if you have a total of 1,000 shares. When you take just 10% off the table it allows you reap in some profits and reduce your risk.

Always take profits into strength as the stock moves in your favor. It's one of the greatest risk management strategies that I have learnt!

You will make more money going long than going short because a stock can only go down to zero.

Stocks can move in a few different ways. They can move up, down, or consolidate. Moves to the upside are the largest moves in a stock since a stock has an infinite upside potential.

When a stock consolidates or bases it moves sideways. Distribution is happening during sideways action for the next move up or down. Consolidation can take six to eight weeks.

Downward moves are fast and don't last a long time. This is where you can make some quick cash if you time it properly because the moves are faster since panic sets in. When trading a stock short, the disadvantage is that stocks can only move down to 0 which usually gives you a smaller risk to reward ratio whereas to the upside there is infinite potential.

Since the moves to the downside are fast and don't last long always be ready for a pop – they can come at any time.

Always measure your reward to your risk before entering a trade.

Before you enter any trade you should know what the reward is to its risk. If you have a stock that has a potential to go up $2, but your stop is $1 - your reward to risk is 2:1.

If you have a stock that has a potential of going $15, but you are only willing to give it a $1 stop then your reward to risk is a 15:1; you are much more likely to gain.

The odds are more in your favor when you have a better ratio. Always watch the ratio of your reward to your risk and make sure you have the better odds.

I always like to make sure I have at least a 5 to 1 reward to my risk. This allows me to be wrong five times and still break even.

You won't fail overnight. Failure is the result of mistakes repeated every day.

One of the main reasons people fail is because they do the same thing expecting different results. That is insanity!

If you are constantly eating fast food at midnight and going to bed at 1:00 AM you might be disappointed with your weight gain eventually when you have a fat belly that was growing every week. Learning from your mistakes quickly is a key to success in anything you do!

When trading in the stock market, the faster you can learn from your own mistakes the better off you will be. As you evolve from each mistake you will continuously improve your trading craft before it becomes a large loss.

The downside is that you have to be consciously aware and honest with yourself about your mistakes. There will always be a time when you don't want to admit your faults. No one will point them out for you and sometimes long term mistakes are not as obvious.

If you want to be successful then find someone who has achieved what you want and do what they do.

Success is pretty simple. You find someone that has achieved what you want to achieve and do what they did. The steps won't be identical, but the type of actions will be similar.

If you want to be a professional actor you may need to start with acting classes. No one starts shooting a box office movie their first time on stage.

If you want to be a successful investor like Warren Buffet then you need to find stocks that will appreciate in value dramatically over the next 10 to 50 years and stick to that plan.

If you want to be a successful trader, then you need to do what successful traders do. Find someone who has achieved what you want, get inside their head, learn their strategies, figure out how they think, and mimic them.

Of course remember to adjust in the process.

When you have experience and you have volatility, you will learn to love the markets!

Volatility is the magnitude of the movement in the markets. If the volatility is high that means the market moves an extreme amount to the upside or downside. Volatility has nothing to do with the direction of the move – it's the amount of movement.

Most beginner traders are scared of volatility because the moves can be wild. One day the swing might be 150+ points in the Dow Jones to the upside and the next day to the down side. When you're a beginner you get scared when the markets are volatile because you don't have the experience.

As you gain experience you will learn to love volatility in the markets because you will be able to catch these crazy moves and capitalize on their profitable movements!

Never get excited or emotional about your stock. The feelings never last long and can kill you later.

Emotions are one of the things that can kill your trading account. If you are emotional about a stock then you are too attached.

Think of this as when you first started dating or a close relationship ended. When you first start dating you don't think clearly because you are in a happy and joyful mood. One day your date is rude - but it's okay because "you are in love." If things don't turn out so well and the relationship ends badly then you feel poorly and think about it.

In both of these instances you are not yourself because your emotions are running the show. Stay clear minded when trading and don't get emotionally attached to stocks because of their company name.

Watch the price and see the results that come from your investment. Trading or investing is a numbers game so stick to the numbers.

When you have a bearish day, always watch which stocks are acting strong and weak.

If you've been watching the markets for at least a year you will definitely go through bearish or down days. When you have bearish days it is a good idea to watch which stocks are acting strong, going up, or going down minimally. Watching which stocks are strong and how they are reacting to the down markets can be like a poker player's tell.

If the stock is acting strong during a down market then they will act even stronger when the market turns around and becomes bullish. Remember that there is never a guarantee that the stock will act strong when the market reverses, but it may shed some light on where the strength is.

Watch them closely.

Be prepared for a stock to come back and retest support levels after a stock breaks higher. Stocks don't go straight up.

I always emphasize that stocks do not go straight up because most people believe they do, or at least they hope they do once they hit the buy button.

Let me tell you something: stocks don't go straight up!

They like to retest support and resistance levels and they follow the path of least resistance.

When stocks test key levels these are great points to add to your position as you learn to spot healthy stock movements.

Catching tops and bottoms is nearly impossible in the stock market.

We all want to catch the top or the bottom in a stock when we are trading. The problem is catching the top or bottom is about as difficult as trying to catch an arrow coming at you at 100 miles per hour. You never know when the top or bottom will come or whens the right time to pull the trigger.

It is better to focus on risk management and proper money management than aiming to hit the highs or the lows.

It is for this reason there is the famous phrase of "don't try to catch a falling knife" because you never know the right place to grab it. Trying to catch a fall stock will hurt you badly.

The better route is to wait for the knife to stick in the ground and then grab it. Which means wait for the stock to find a base then you can pull the trigger.

Stock operators will pump a stock into the market so they can sell you their shares. Don't buy their hype.

There are many stock operators out there who control a large part of any given stock. It takes them months to build up a position in a stock because they are accumulating shares.

When these people want to sell their shares they like to build hype and pump up a company. Think about the famous Carl Icahn tweet that moved Apple's stock over 18+ points. They do these tricks so they can sell their shares to you because they have such a large position it takes time for them to get out! This is how the game is played!

P.S. Here is the famous tweet link:
https://twitter.com/Carl_C_Icahn/statuses/367350206993399808

It only takes a few stocks to make your year. You don't have to trade hundreds of companies.

After trading for quite a while I noticed that I tend to trend the same companies repeatedly. I've learned how they move, act, and behave. Most people stick to companies they are familiar with. Every stock has a certain rhythm to their movement.

The better you are at finding this rhythm (similar to finding a dance rhythm) the more likely you are to succeed. When you know this rhythm like the back of your hand you will have a greater advantage over the other traders who have only looked at a stock a handful of times.

Earnings can burn you!
Don't ever hold a stock through earnings.

If you are a trader then you should never hold a stock through earnings! Earnings can and will burn you!

Yes there is the potential of a stock gapping up 10% or 20%, but why would you give back all your gains? It makes no sense! Most of the time earnings will burn you because you never know which way a stock will move.

If you do decide to trade during earnings on a stock that you held as a winner over the last few months, then sell 90% of your holdings and let 10% of your position ride. In my mind this would be called "gambling cautiously." Otherwise do not trade through earnings!

P.S. The only time to hold through earnings is when you are a long term investor planning to hold the company for years.

If things look blurry and you aren't in the market then wait 30 minutes to allow the market to show you a direction.

When you first open your trading screens in the morning and the market just opened - sometimes there is no clear direction.

If you don't know which direction the market is heading just wait 30 minutes for the market to show you where it wants to go. You don't have to be the first one in. What's the rush?

There are times where you may even have to sit out of the markets for weeks or months to find the direction and energy of the markets.

You don't have to be in a trade every single day of the year. You just have capitalize on the returns when the opportunity presents itself. If you make your year in three months then you can take the rest of the year off and enjoy your time with your family or go travel. Live a little!

Don't invest in hope and prayer. It doesn't pay well with investments.

You can hope and pray all you want with your stock trades, but the returns are usually horrible if you base your trading decisions on hope and prayer.

The main problem with the hope and prayer tactic is that many other people are praying opposite of what you are praying for. You never know which prayers will get answered first.

Hope and prayer can work wonderfully for many things in life, but not the stock market. When it comes to your investments it is better to stick to a proven system and a trading plan when you are dealing with your money.

Leave the higher powers to deal with other areas of life.

Don't get hyped up about technology or shiny objects. They will only distract you while trading.

There's always something new that's coming out especially in the tech world. Just like in the real world people want a new phone, tablet, or that next technical gadget. In the trading world people want the new newest software or the Holy Grail trading indicator.

People want the latest indicator that will solve all their trading problems. They want a new trading platform that's faster and quicker by just a micro second. In fact, I get more questions about my software than money management.

We are always going after the shiny objects that will do very little to our trading. Stick to the basics and fundamentals. Focus on proven risk and money management strategies. Learn from your mistakes and study past history to evolve yourself to the next level. This will add more value to you than looking after that next hottest charting platform.

Never allow a trade to turn into an investment.

Stocks are not always predictable. If you have a stock that you are taking for a trade-only (meaning just for the day or that week) then you need to stick to your plan.

I find that if things get sour and the stock goes against you, beginner traders will add to the position and continue to add over the next few weeks in hopes of making their money back.

If you continue to add to a position years can go by and you might be left with thousands of shares of bad stock. Some stocks take years to recover and others never recover.

Stick to your plan and don't allow a trade that you were planning to hold for just a week or two turn into a lifetime investment.

The opportunity cost is expensive!

Never trade on margin or leverage until you have proven rules, a system, and a track record.

In the beginning of our trading career we get very excited with the power that we have at our finger tips. When we discover that we can trade on margin or even trade options to make more money it can be a very enticing.

If you don't have a proven record, a system that works, and trading rules that you stick with then you should not trade on margin or use leverage!

By using margin or leverage you are adding to your risk. There's no reason to add more risk to your trades unless you know how the game is played and you have a proven track record. Instead what you will do is lose more money faster!

Stay away from margin and leverage until you are profitable for at least one year.

Markets & stocks will correct. They usually take 6 to 8 weeks. Be patient and sit on the sidelines or learn to trade short.

All markets will correct eventually. You need to be prepared for them and always watch for the start of the correction which will allow you to make adjustments to your trades and portfolio sooner rather than later.

Corrections take time and don't happen overnight. We often want them to happen quickly so that we can get back to the act of making trades. However corrections usually last 6 to 8 weeks. If a correction is taking place you need to learn to trade short or sit in cash until the clouds clear.

There is nothing in the rule book that says you have to trade every day. Be patient and wait for the right opportunity.

Never buy a large gap up in an over-bought market, the same way that you wouldn't chase a stock that is up $10+ dollars in a day.

When stocks gap up, never chase it! Typically stocks like to retest their breakout points and this is why gaps "typically" get filled. When there is an empty region where no trades took place it sucks the momentum and energy of the stock.

It's similar to a magnet attracting another magnet or a piece of metal.

If you want to trade gaps the better route is to "fade the gap" which means trading it to the short side. Otherwise don't chase gap ups in stocks because they can retrace and you will hit your stops.

Brushing your teeth 14 times on Monday doesn't work. Some things you have to do every day.

If you want to have great teeth you need to brush your teeth every single day. You can't just wake up on Monday and say – "Okay – it's Monday so I'm going to brush my teeth fourteen times today." This method doesn't work well for your oral care.

If you want to become a great stock trader or make money consistently from this craft you have to put the time and study into it every single day.

You can't just wake up once a month and say "Today I'm going to trade stocks and make money." If you've been doing it for 40+ years professionally you might be able to, but in theory it's a bad approach.

Nevertheless at the beginning you need to practice and improve your game daily. Only then will you be a greater trader.

Always watch the second day for confirmation.

When a stock breaks out of a range always watch the second day for a confirmation. If the stock is moving well the second day and continues to follow through then the stock is acting strong and you have your confirmation. If its acting weak or continues lower it might be better to step aside.

Remember that stocks often like to come back and retest their break out levels. So don't panic if your stock retraces to retest support after the first day.

Never allow a winning trade to turn into losing trade.

I often see many people entering a stock at the right time, but so many of them fail to take profits and reduce their risk when a stock goes in their favor.

If you have a stock that is a winning trade and moved in your favor, never allow it to turn into a losing trade because it will burn you! Remember that stocks can change direction at any time.

Too many people allow their stock go back to their entry after they were profitable. It then turns into a $200 loss, $1,000 loss, or even a $5,000 loss until the pain is so large that they are forced to sell or forced to hold.

That's why you never allow a winning trade to turn into a losing trade.

If a stock is pushing higher toward the end of the day then it is showing strength.

Stocks that continue to run up as the trading day comes to a close show strength. It is at these times where you can hold your position overnight for a swing trade. Of course if you want to reduce your risk then you can sell part of your position.

If your stock is selling off towards the end of the day then it showing weakness. This is when you want to be careful holding a position overnight especially if you just entered it.

The same is true if you are short. If you are short and a stock continues to selloff further into the close then it is showing more weakness giving you confirmation on your short position.

If a stock is not acting right you don't have to wait for it to hit your stop.

Not every trade will work out in your favor. In fact you will have many losing trades. As you get better at spotting the action and the movement of your stocks you will learn to see when things just don't look right.

If things don't look right then you don't have to wait for your stock to hit your stop!

Why wait and give up more of your profits? Get out if something doesn't look right. You can always get back in later and possibly at a cheaper price.

If a stock is making higher highs on lighter volume take your money or prepare for a huge down draft.

A healthy move for a stock is when you see it going up on heavy volume and retracing on lighter volume.

Stocks that are making higher highs on lighter volume typically have a stronger pull back when it happens. The reason is there is limited conviction and the movement has only a little bit of juice behind it.

The higher and longer a stock goes up on lighter volume the stronger the pullback. This doesn't mean you cannot trade low volume movers. It just means be more cautious and take profits as the stock moves in your favor. It also means be prepared to act quickly when necessary.

P.S. Stocks don't move in a straight line – we should expect retracements. A healthy move for a bearish stock is when it is moving down on heavy volume and moving up on lighter volume.

The large institutions and the big boys move the markets not the individual investor. Pay attention to what they are doing!

When you are trading stocks, especially companies over $20+ dollars, it is the big institutions that move the markets. Watch what they are doing by watching the charts and their holdings and you will see their game plan unfold.

Just remember to never listen to what they say because they will always try to fake you out to buy their shares or tell you to sell so they can buy your shares.

The news is there to report exciting things. It doesn't mean you need to trade the stocks they are talking about.

When I first got into trading I would make trading decisions based on the news - that was a very bad idea! Remember that the financial channels and news broadcasts are there to report the interesting and juicy stuff. They are looking for audience retention so that they can make money from channel sponsorships and advertisers.

Although it can be a great place to find out what's moving or hear about the active stocks, don't trade the stocks being discussed on TV solely because they are on TV. Learn to do your own homework and research so that you can make your own trading decisions.

You will never be a consistent trader if you follow someone blindly.

There are thousands of traders out there that you can follow, get their stock alerts, and get trade ideas. All of them have their own trading style and what works for them. If you are looking for someone to help evolve your trading then you need to find someone you can relate to. Don't just follow someone blindly and copy their trades.

Learn why they are trading the stocks they are. Figure out what they are looking for. Then mimic them and their success so you can be successful on your own.

If you just follow someone blindly (including me), then you will never learn how to trade on your own. You will always need someone to hold your hand and show you which stock to trade. Imagine what will happen to your portfolio when they quit sharing their trades or die? You will be helpless...

Most people follow lagging indicators. This is why they always are late to the party. Learn to read volume and you will be ahead of most people.

I often get questions about what indicators I use besides volume and although I do use a handful at a very specific time most of the time I ignore them. However everyone always asks what they are because they think they are a magic formula for predicting the future. The fact is most of the lagging indicators suck! That's why they are called *lagging indicators.*

The best indicator to watch is volume! When you learn to spot quality volume you will know when to pull the trigger. Volume will tell you if a stock is healthy and what's happening. Volume is real-time so there is no lag between the indicator's signal and your entry when you watch volume. If you are waiting for the lagging indicators to make your trade decisions or entries you will be late and miss the trade.

It's never easy to sell when you have a loss. Be disciplined to admit to your faults and it will get easier over time.

Would you rather have a 7000 paper cuts or have one of your legs cut off? I would take the paper cuts any day. I can recover from them eventually.

One of the greatest problems we humans have is saying "I lost" or "I failed." Since we want to avoid pain we tend to not want to admit we have a losing trade. Unfortunately, losing trades continue to grow and the pain becomes bigger over time until we can't handle it and are forced to sell or hold because we over-leveraged.

Be quick to take your paper cuts so can you recover from them. If you get stuck in a trade that will take off your limb it is dangerous and a very difficult recovery.

Stocks do not go straight up or straight down.
This is why it is difficult for many people.
They have corrections and basing patterns.

The ideal situation right after we buy a stock is that it continues to head higher. Unfortunately this doesn't happen that often. Stocks go through three main phases. They move higher, they base and consolidate, and they have pull backs.

Most people want the stock to immediately start heading higher after they buy it, but it doesn't always work that way. Be patient for your stock to build the momentum to make the move when it's ready.

Usually the strongest time of the year for stocks is Thanksgiving through Christmas. Play the market according to the action you see.

The market has its own breath. Think of it like a living breathing organism that mimics human behavior. Historically the strongest time of the year for the market has been Thanksgiving to Christmas.

This is because companies are able to see how profitable they are for the year, bonuses are distributed, and people feel happier during the holidays. All these things create optimism.

Watch the market action during the holiday season because it usually moves well allowing you to capture great returns and can make your year in a short trading period.

Don't create a circus of indicators on your trading screens. Keep things simple.

Novice traders often want to add the newest and latest indicator they just discovered to their screen. Adding more indicators and signals does not mean you will be a better trader or make more money.

If you have 30 different signals going off at different times of the day then which signal are you really watching and listening to?

I love how the Dollar Shave Club commercial relates to this concept. You don't need to have a razor that has a backscratcher, massager, and 20 blades. You just need something that shaves well.

On your stock chart you don't need 50+ indicators – you just need the right signal to tell you when to enter.

The stock market is a game of inventory. Know which produce is going bad and get rid of it.

If you think about running a business selling fruit then you know that you should sell and get rid of the fruit that is going bad first. The more fruit you can move and get rid of before it spoils the better off your business will be. If your fruit has fruit flies and starts to rot then no one will want it.

Think how this applies to stocks. If you have five (5) stocks and 4 are doing great and on one (1) you are losing money, then you should get rid of the bad fruit and hold on to the great inventory.

Start thinking about your portfolio as your inventory and it might shift your paradigm. Keep around the best stuff as long as you can.

Education takes time, energy, and money. Which resource do you have the most of?

When you are learning anything whether you are studying in college or learning to trade – it chews up your resources. Education takes your time, energy, and money.

You have to put the time into something if you want to learn it. We can't insert a chip program in your brain like the Matrix and out comes this amazing human that knows how to trade perfectly.

You need to put the energy into learning to trade. This means you give a part of you either your time, emotions, or dedication. Just because you put some time into watching videos doesn't mean you will get the results – that's why you need energy!

Money is the last thing that is required to learn to trade. You are going to pay for your education in some way. This can be from buying video courses, books, or learn the hard way from costly trading mistakes.

All three of these components make up your education. The resource that you have the most of is the one that you should use to your advantage. If you have more money, you may want to purchase someone to coach you. However if you have more time you might want to study anything and everything you can get your hands on. Use the resource that you have the most of.

You can't wish for things to be easier. Instead wish that you were better.

Everyone wants things to be easier. I wished for things to be given to me on a silver platter – it never came. People want this not only in the markets, but in life. They want skills for putting no time or effort into themselves. Instead of wishing that things were easier for you - wish that you were better!

When it comes to stock trading, things will never be easier with the markets. In fact they get more difficult because the more people know about the markets the more the game changes. You will have to constantly improve your game.

So instead of wishing for things to be easier wish that you were better. Think about how you can take your trading to the next level.

When there is an IPO operators will pump the stock into the market only to sell you their shares. Don't buy their hype.

IPO's can be exciting especially for new traders. They come with a lot of hype. There are a lot of press releases, articles, TV coverage, and blogs that cover the stories. However most of the time an IPO or even the first few months a company is public is a terrible time to get into a stock.

The reason they are so terrible to get into at the beginning is you have a lot of investors that got into the company much earlier before it was even public. They are looking to capitalize on their investment and sell their shares into you. That's why they hype up and pump up the company because they are looking to dump their shares.

Look at companies like Tesla or Facebook where it took a few months to consolidate until the stocks finally got going. If you are interested in an IPO or a newly traded company allow the charts to setup for a few months and prove to you that it has some stability. Otherwise you might be left with bad stock that will never rise.

Stock leaders are usually the first to go. They lead the market lower and they lead the market higher.

Always watch the leading companies in the stock market. They are leaders due to their liquidity because they are the easiest to get in and out of. Stock leaders move to the upside first before the rest of the market moves higher. This is what it means when they say "the leaders lead the market higher."

In addition, the leaders move the markets lower. If you start seeing leaders turning negative for a few days, but the small caps are moving higher it usually means the rest of the market will roll over soon and follow the leaders.

Leaders lead the markets higher and they lead the markets lower.

If a stock has moved $10+ dollars in a single day - don't chase it.

Often times when we are scanning charts during the day we notice a stock that has broken out, but sadly it is at a much higher price than what we wanted to pay. One thing to live by is not to chase things.

This motto applies to chasing women and the same is true for stocks. Allow everything to flow naturally rather than forcing a trade you didn't intend to make.

If you chase a stock that is $100+ per share and is already up $10+ dollars in a day then it has moved quite a bit. You are better off to wait for a pull back. The risk is against you.

If you are trading stocks between $30 and $100 then if a stock is up $5+ then again don't chase it. Remember that there is always another trade out there. Find the best ones.

When there is uncertainty in Washington the markets will be choppy and whipsaw around. There is nothing wrong with staying in cash.

There are certain days or weeks where there is uncertainty in Washington or with the Government. This could be anything from the monetary policy to the Presidents health or a Senate hearing. If things are uncertain in Washington the markets will be choppier than usual. You don't have to trade during these times. Just sit out until things clear up and you figure out a direction.

Understand the vehicle you are trading before entering the trade. Stocks, ETF's, and options all move differently.

Trading the same stocks will ensure better consistency because you will know how these stocks behave, when they breakout, and how they move during news events. Stocks mimic human behavior and people typically trade the same stocks over their lifetime.

As you start moving into different asset classes or trades, you need to adjust your trading system. Just as if you were playing tennis with kids vs. adults you would probably adjust your playing style to the other player whether you want to win against the adults or allow the kids to enjoy themselves and have fun.

Stocks, ETF's, and options all move differently and you need to take note when trading these investment classes. Don't trade options the same way you would trade stocks. Even if you trade only stocks, you would not trade penny stocks or stocks under $5 the same way that you would trade stocks that are $300 or $500 like the Googles or Apples of the market. Know what you are trading and adjust accordingly.

When you trade a stock, don't worry if the company makes umbrellas or raincoats. Just trade the stock.

Too many people fall in love with their stock or the company that they trade. I have seen it many times with Apple as it was dropping in 2013 people held on to the stock screaming "it's Apple!" Let's not forget people said the same thing about Enron.

Don't fall in love with your stock. It won't cuddle you at night. I don't care if a stock sells toilet paper, umbrellas, or raincoats – just trade the stocks that are moving appropriately and stick to your trading rules.

Stock trading is about risk and money management. It's not just about picking the hottest stocks.

Most novice traders are always thinking about the next hottest stock. The fact is stock trading isn't just about picking hot stocks. This is part of the game, but probably the less important part. The more important part to learn about risk and money management.

If you know risk and money management and you are picking the wrong stocks you will survive and keep your account in good shape. If you are a great stock picker, but have horrible risk and money management you will kill your account. Focus on the important things when it comes to trading.

Setup your risk and reward strategy before entering any trade.

Before you get into a trade always have a plan! Think like professional chess player that thinks 10, 20, or 50 moves ahead. They are planning for the "what if" situations that may come up.

If you plan for various things that may happen with the stock movement or the effect it can have on your position you will trade calmer and have an edge. Don't ever enter a trade without having a risk-reward strategy or a trading plan.

When stocks sell off on bad news this is a sign of bearish sentiment in the market. Watch it closely.

If stocks are selling of on bad news this shows negativity in the markets. This means that bad news is making them flinch and run for cover. If this happens it is telling you that the market was being held up by air.

I've seen markets go up when there were disasters happening. The news broadcasters showed crazy footage and stocks were still acting strong. Of course the level of severity is key to watch, but if markets sell off on common everyday bad news then they are acting weak. When weakness comes step aside until things have a chance to digest.

If the market is buying on bad news, this is a sign of a bullish market. Learn to read the subtle signs and you will have a trading edge.

There will always be some kind of negative thing happening in the markets. This is why there are always bulls and bears. If everyone was bullish or bearish then the markets would not move.

The markets move because there is this imbalance effect. When the market is buying on bad news then more people are looking to become bullish and this is a positive sign for the markets.

Support and resistance lines are not perfect. Stocks won't bounce or reverse at precise areas. There is confluence involved.

Most people want support or resistance areas to be perfect and precise, but the markets don't work like this. Everyone is always trying to buy it at the lowest price and sell at the highest. Larger stocks like to wiggle much more so you need to give them more room to bounce around and find their meeting point (which is confluence).

Think about it if you were to meet a friend at a restaurant at 6:00 you don't show up at exactly 6:00. Typically they may show up at 5:58 or you might show up at 6:02. They may wait for you inside or outside. However, you find each other. The exact meeting point might be at a table because your friend might be sitting down as you show up. This is called confluence. It is the meeting or joining point.

The timing or location when you meet someone isn't perfect, but it gives you a rough guideline just like with support and resistance lines.

A stock won't move right after you hit the buy order. You need to have patience. Thousands of other people hope for the same thing throughout the day.

We all want things to happen immediately after we hit the buy button. We want that stock to continue to fly to the moon. This is an unrealistic expectation. When trading you might not have a perfect entry just like you won't buy at the lows and sell at the highs. Instead you need to buy the stocks that are acting and behaving correctly.

So don't expect a stock to take off and blast higher after you pull the trigger because thousands of other people were hoping for the same thing weeks or months earlier. Remember to buy right and sit tight.

Do not get married to any stock because of what they do.

When we love a company's products, we fall in love with the company. This happens in companies like Apple where people stand for days for the latest iPhone release only to get it weeks before other people.

This can be a dangerous characteristic to have when you are trading a company's stock. Don't fall in love with a company just because of what they do.

If everything is screaming out that the company is tanking and losing money it is best to cut your losses than to attach yourself with the beauty of the company's products.

Remember that the stock market leads the retail world and eventually the company will follow.

If a stock gaps down hard on heavy volume step aside. It takes weeks and months for things to rebuild. Some stocks never come back.

You will see stocks gapping up or down frequently the more involved you are in the markets. If a stock is gapping down hard on heavy volume this is a bearish sign and a huge red flag! Step aside and take your position off for safety reasons.

Don't pray and hope for a stock to come back because sometimes they never come back. Some stocks stay under $5 or $10 bucks after one major event. It may take years for it to recover.

Always have a trading plan for each trade and for your account.

Many beginner traders enter stocks because "they look good" or they like the company. They have no plan for their trade nor do they have a plan for their overall account.

Before you start trading always have a plan for each trade that you put on. What will you do if the stock goes up $10 or goes down $5?

In addition, have a plan for your overall account. When will you take money off the table and put it into your bank? When will you take a vacation or add money to your account? Having some plan is better than no plan at all.

It is never about the news, but the reaction to the news.

Various stocks make the news every single day. Most news is just broadcasted because it gets attention or something to keep you reading or watching. Remember they are in it for the viewership.

You don't need to worry about what is being said on the news. Instead you need to watch the reaction of your stocks to the news. Always watch how your stocks are acting and behaving to different kinds of news. Are they acting strong during negative news? Are they acting weak during positive news? Watch the reaction – don't worry about what is being said. Most news is just hype and what someone thinks anyways.

Watch how a stock comes into various swing points and it will tell you the strength.

Stocks will often test and retest swing points, lines of support, and lines of resistance. Watch the price, action, and volume of how they come into these swing points. The more volume and speed along with proper movement (behavior) the more likely it will break.

If a stock isn't acting right and moving sluggish into a swing point then chances are it will bounce. Watch the swing points and study them as they will create great opportunities to add to your positions.

Learn to trade on your own information and your own methods. It is the only way you will be successful!

When you take trades from other people and do what they do without understanding why they take the trade - then you are setting yourself up for failure!

Every trader (experienced ones for that matter), look at many different trades and hold them for different length. Some trades are for short term and others are long term investments. When you see what stocks other people are talking about you need still follow your own guidelines and rules.

If you don't, then you can never improve your trading because you won't spot where you made mistakes. Doing this will make you very inconsistent since you will rely on other people.

So stick to your own plan and trade on your own information. It doesn't mean you can't get alerts from other traders, but it does mean you need to have your own plan when you put on your trades.

Most upgrades and downgrades on stocks are setup to suck you in. Don't buy their hype!

There are many people that go on TV that talk about stocks being either bullish or bearish, but there is a reason that there are regulations that force them to disclose if they hold the stock they are discussing.

It is because some people lie and manipulate others so that they can do things for their own agenda!

Be careful when listening to what people say on TV about various stocks. It's never a good thing when your future is riding based on what someone else said.

When someone on TV tells you to buy the stock, they are trying to sell it to you. If they are telling you to SELL the stock, they missed the move and want to buy your shares.

All too often novice traders look to the TV experts for their trading ideas or to figure out which way a stock will go. Many of the people on TV are traders themselves and managing a huge portfolio. They are looking out for themselves first, their company second, and then maybe you.

Most of the time if they tell you to buy the stock then they are getting ready to sell it. If they are telling you the stock will go down then they want to accumulate and buy more of your shares at a lower price. This is how the game of manipulation is played. Don't buy their hype!

When you are long in a stock and its moving well allow it to run as much as possible. Don't be too quick to take your profits.

If you've entered a stock and you are on the right side of the trade sometimes it can be exciting to watch your profits rising. One of the greatest tips I can give you is "be patient."

Beginners often want to take their money quickly only to discover 30 minutes later (or 2 days later) that the stock continues higher and then they continue to beat themselves up over it.

If the stock is acting right and moving well then be patient and allow things to continue to move. Then slowly take your profits when you start seeing some weakness – or exit immediately when the sentiment changes.

If there is news coming from the Federal Reserve (FED) the market will be choppy. Allow the market to show you its hand before trading.

The Federal Reserve adjusts rates and how much money they print. If there is news that is something coming out from the Fed (let's say at noon or sometime this week) then be patient as the markets like to beat around the bush and speculate as to what will happen.

No one knows what will happen so it is better to enter once the market shows you its hand. Until the FED releases a statement the markets can whipsaw around. Remember that someone always knows more.

Stocks can move much higher or lower than you expect. Be patient and allow things to setup.

Traders often try to anticipate a stock price movement and how low it can go then aim to buy it at the lowest price only to find out that it wasn't the lowest price.

As the famous saying goes, trying to catch a stock that is moving lower quickly is like trying to catch a falling knife. Stocks can move much lower than you think or expect. Your mind will play tricks on you and tease you when to get in.

Be patient and allow things to confirm the bounce or up movement in your stock before purchasing it.

The same is true on the upside if you are trying to short. Certain stocks can run much higher than you expect so be patient when trying to short. You don't have to be the first one in – otherwise you will be the biggest sucker.

"The average man doesn't wish to be told that it is a bull or a bear market. What he desires is to be told specifically which particular stock to buy or sell. He wants to get something for nothing. He does not wish to work. He doesn't even wish to have to think."
– Jesse Livermore

I love this quote from Jesse Livermore. I think that people rely too much on trading alert websites to trade rather than learning things themselves or using the website as a tools.

I find that the people who want the picks eventually they will want you to trade their account for them. They want everything for nothing – don't be one of these people.

After you trade their account they will say they want you to make them more money. It never ends. Learn to put the time, effort, and energy into doing your own homework. That's how you become successful!

It isn't the markets that beat people, but people beat themselves with the markets.

The market is constantly moving. It moves up, down, and sideways. Although most people think that the market beats them, if you look at the bigger picture people beat themselves with the markets.

As traders, we typically enter the wrong type of trades at the wrong time. We are excited to get into the market when there is just a slight pop. We don't focus on our risk, but tend to focus on our potential profits.

It is for these actions and many others that people get smacked upside the head by the markets. It is because we do the wrong things at the wrong time, get greedy, excited, or are fearful that the market takes us on a ride.

Never dollar-cost average down if your stock is moving lower. It will only burn you later!

All too often I have seen many traders leave the business because of one simple mentality - they want to dollar cost average and buy more stock when they are down. I think this has to do with two primary reasons.

The first one being that they don't want to take a loss or admit that they were wrong. They feel that they can save the trade or make up for it. The second is that too many regular financial gurus who do not understand risk management or trading stocks say things like "if McDonalds keeps going down do you think that it will go under? Just keep buying more..."

I would say that in theory this principle is right, but I can think of a few instances like GM, Lehman Brothers, and Enron that got delisted off the stock exchange and millions of people lost thousands of dollars. The choice is up to you, but in my opinion it is better to take the loss and buy the stock back later at a lower price than keep adding money into a losing trade.

All tipsters in the stock market are right, but most are wrong when it comes down to the "when."

If you've been in the markets for some time and interacted with other traders then you know that markets isolate. Some days it goes up and other days it goes down and so many people chat and discuss where the next move will be.

These tipsters who watch the market and predict the future of various stocks are all correct in their predictions. They are all correct because the market isolates. Eventually it pulls back and sometimes it powers higher. The more important question to ask when hearing these tips is what is the time frame?

The tipster's outlook on the market view may be only 20 minutes. For other people it could be 20 years. You need to recognize that what someone says may not apply to you directly. You have to trade your plan according to your strategy.

A tip is only as good as the execution.

Stocks will go to the place where there is least resistance just as water does running down a mountain.

There are always buyers and sellers in every market. The stock market moves in the same way as water. It moves where the energy pushes it, which means to the place where there is the least resistance.

Think of it as water running down a mountain or waterfall. The gravity pushes the water lower until it reaches its lowest point or until the resistance is so great that it gets evaporated back up.

If a stock is moving up that means that there is not that many sellers above these price points to push the stock lower. There are more buyers to push the stock higher. Since there are more buyers pushing the stock higher there is less resistance above and that's why the stock goes up.

It's all about the path of least resistance in the same way that humans want things – the easy way.

Always track your trades and emotions in a trading journal. It will be one of your greatest learning tools.

If you track anything you probably love to track your profits. You might hate to track your losses. If you get more into tracking things and enjoy seeing progress, start writing down your own emotions during the trading day at the open, at lunch time, and at the close as you execute trades.

Having a trading journal or a way to track trades is important. However, tracking your emotions and things that are usually not well measured can be exceptionally beneficial to the trader who is self-aware.

You can track the quality of your emotions, calmness, mental clarity, etc. with smiley faces or letter grades – the important part is to self-reflect.

You will learn more from losing trades than winning trades. Keep your education as cheap as possible.

When learning any kind of craft or business it costs money. This could be your tools of the craft, fees for tuition, or the cost of your education from your mistakes.

Novice traders want to pile in a heap of their money right from the start because they believe they will be successful. However what they quickly discover is that their trading is poor (it may be they don't want to admit to it).

Rather than putting in a large amount of money into trading from the beginning it is better to trade lightly. This could be with just a few shares or contracts until you build some experience. After all you don't want to run a 50 mile marathon race if you never ran before. It might be better to start out with a 5 mile race, 15 mile race, or even a 25 mile race. You don't just go for a 50 mile marathon without practice and training.

Make your education as cheap as possible by trading just a few shares or contracts. It may be that your commissions hurt you, but the goal is to learn from your losing trades and your mistakes. Once you've gotten most of your dumb mistakes out of the way as cheaply as possible, to increase your profits all you have to do is hit a different button on the keyboard.

It's that easy.

Big losses are expensive! Take your losses as small as possible when the pain is the smallest.

We often get attached to our stocks once we buy them. Buying is easy. It is taking a loss that is hard – hard on your account and your psychology. If you learn to take your losses small, when the pain is minimal, then you can recover.

Let's say you were stuck in an interrogation prison. Would you rather someone whips you on your back or cut off your limb? I'm sure you would definitely take the whipping because you can recover from it. If your limb is cut off then the recovery is minimal and life would be more difficult.

Unfortunately when people trade they hold on to losses much longer than they should and they end up cutting off a body part such as a finger, a hand, or an arm. This makes it very tough for your account to recover from these extreme losses. So never cut off your limbs when trading stocks. Take losses as fast as possible so you can recover quickly.

You can be successful in the stock market if you are intelligent, willing to put the effort into it, and treat it like a business. Unfortunately, most never do what is necessary – so they are not successful.

I love it when people ask me "how long does it take to be successful in the stock market?" I never know anyone well enough to assess this from my readers. I don't know how long they studied, how much time they put in, and their mentality. Now my coaching students are a different story since we have a deeper relationship.

If you study, you will attain a lot of knowledge but you may not do anything with it. When you study AND you put the effort into testing strategies to see what works then you may get results that you can interpret. However this doesn't mean you will be successful.

Once you start changing your behavior based on the results that you get – this is when you start seeing the success at the end of the tunnel. It will give you a glimpse into what is possible. Most people will never be successful because they may only do half of what's needed to get where they want to be.

Learn to watch other markets like the FTSE & DAX. Remember we are a global economy.

In today's world we have become a global economy. It is important for you to recognize this phenomenon and watch what happens to other markets around the world. You don't have to follow them every inch or tick, but checking on them once a week is a good idea.

I like to check them once a day depending on the conditions because if we have a sell off overseas with the London markets it may pull the US markets lower.

Remember that London trades ahead of the US markets by nearly half a day so it gives you a great preview of what's to come. It isn't a crystal ball or guaranteed that it will work every single time, but it could give you an insight if there are serious problems in the world economy.

When you accumulate stock always buy it on an incline not on a decline.

If you are a looking for a long term position and looking to accumulate stock over the long haul then make sure you purchase stock as it is moving in your favor and acting right.

Figure out what price area is a good accumulation place for you and then start buying at that area. Then make sure you stick to your profit and loss targets. If a stock drops below your price area or region that you set in place then you need to get out..

You should always have a plan whether it is for long term trades or short term trades. Just because you plan to accumulate a certain stock for the long term this doesn't mean you have to be naive to neglect huge market drops or be in denial if a company is behaving badly.

Patterns repeat in the markets because markets are driven by humans. Learn to find the patterns.

If you wonder why markets have cycles or repeat it's because they operate on human behavior and human behavior repeats. We typically get into loop cycles repeating our routines or daily activities and the same with the stock market, but in a longer wave cycle.

Since there are patterns and cycles that repeat it makes the market *somewhat* predictable. If you can learn to spot the patterns then you will be able to take advantage of opportunities that present themselves.

Not every pattern will work out perfectly so it is important you stick to your trading system, but the probabilities will be in your favor once you can read the trends and the patterns - so study them.

Watch the currencies and the dollar because the stock market doesn't like a strong dollar.

If you are a trader or an investor then you need to understand how your stock or investments move as the dollar rises or falls.

Typically commodity and energy stocks (this includes oil and gold companies), do not like a strong dollar. So if you see a potential for the dollar to rise over the next six months then you may want to avoid commodity and energy stocks - or at least be cautious about them.

Of course a strong dollar can be a prideful thing for the country because it makes traveling abroad cheaper due to the exchange rates, but companies with a lot of overseas exposure and sales want the dollar to be weak against other currencies. This makes exporting cheaper and more attractive to foreign buyers.

Since the stock market deals with a lot of huge companies that deal with international business, it is for this reason that they don't like the strong dollar. So watch the dollar closely and how it affects your stocks.

Never forget the greatest stock market crashes of all time. There is always one around the corner.

Stock crashes like the Great Depression from way back when to the flash crashes where the stock market goes down 1000 points in one day do happen!

If you look into your research on the history of the stock market crashes over the last 100+ years you will notice that there isn't just one or two crashes, but at least twenty of them.

They come around when you least expect them. Always be prepared for the next huge down drop because crashes do happen and there is always one around the corner. You just can never see which corner.

If you follow someone, learn why they are buying a stock instead of just following them blindly.

Don't ever follow anyone blindly when you are trading. Learn their system, why they pick the stocks they do, what they are watching, or just get ideas so that you can make your own trading decisions. When you follow someone blindly you will be dependent on them and you never know when they will stop broadcasting their picks.

If you constantly go to the store to buy fish you will never learn how to catch a fish on your own. Worst of all, if you get stuck on a desert island you may starve to death if you don't figure out how to fish quickly.

Stick to limit orders as much as possible. Market orders can damage your profits.

One of the things that I think I was always fairly good at when I first started trading was to use limit orders. Many times you will get filled poorly if you use market orders.

Market orders are fantastic when there's a stock that's moving very quickly and you need to get in as fast as possible. The reason for this is typically you don't want to miss the move. You can also use market orders on things that are very liquid such as ETF's that have millions of shares traded every day.

Beyond those circumstances I would stick to limit orders. If you don't stick to limit orders the swings in the prices and the bid ask spread could kill a great deal of your profits.

Stay patient when entering trades. You don’t have to be the first one through the door. Usually there is always a pullback and you can get in it at that time.

At the end of the day before the market closes always do a fire drill with your position.

Since stocks and the market can do anything it wants to do there is no true security when you are trading or managing your positions.

Before you end the day with open positions in your portfolio you should always do a fire drill to evaluate your risk.

Look at each one of your open positions and see how a gap up or a gap down would affect your profit and loss. When you watch your risk and keep it under control you will become a better trader.

Most people are the opposite and wonder about the potential profits and what they can buy with them (like a jet-ski or fancy car) than their risk.

FREE 30 DAY TRIAL TO THE CRITICAL CHARTS

If you want to see more charts similar to the ones in this book during the current market conditions then you may want to visit www.tradersfly.com and look at acquiring access to my critical charts membership.

I typically try to post a few times a month to show you stocks that are moving, support or resistance lines to watch, or stocks that may breakout or breakdown. It is a great resource to study so that you can continue to practice your chart reading skills.

If you have never signed up to the critical charts before, you are welcome to join me and try the critical chart service for 30 days absolutely free by visiting the following link in your browser window:

http://www.bit.ly/chartfreebies

Once you are there, click the "sign up" button and register for the service. You will get a free 30 day trial to the critical charts.

If you choose to continue receiving access to the critical charts, you do not have to do anything and you will be billed $12 per month, but if you decide not to keep the service you can cancel anytime.

HELP ANOTHER PERSON?

If this book has helped you or you think you can shed some light to others by giving your input, a little background, and insight, then please share your thoughts and do a review on Amazon.

You know there are typically two kinds of reviews. Reviews where people love the book and ones that hate the book. If you study human psychology the reason for this is because we either want to get closer to something and associate with it or get away from something and disassociate.

However, even if you had a neutral feeling then please share your perspective to give other people that may be interested in reading the book your point of view.

I am sure they would appreciate the additional insight from you and of course I thank you as well!

BON VOYAGE

Thanks for reading, studying, and learning from this book. Continue to learn and practice your trading skills. It takes time to develop any skill and it doesn't happen overnight. Be patient, be persistent and you will get exactly what you want.

Here are a few website resources I have that you can check out.

- http://tradersfly.com : Free video lessons and training material on stock trading
- http://rise2learn.com : List of all the courses and trainings I have made are listed here.
- http://sashaevdakov.com : My personal website. See all my training for business, stock trading, and finance.

If you have any questions, comments, or suggestions for future courses or training material feel free to contact me through one of my websites above.

Thanks again,

Sasha

Sasha Evdakov

Made in the USA
Middletown, DE
14 November 2016